Ernest Asamoah-Yaw, Author.

4

Photos

Picture # 1:

    a) Bonwire village center

    b) Starched cotton yarns spread in sun to dry.

    c) A 14yr. old boy at the village using a locally-made spool to spin white-yarn on ribbon

    d) A teenager lining up a set of white-ribbons on pedestal to form a warp onto the loom

    e) A weaver feeding warped threads into **(kyereye)** a woofing instrument

    f) A typical youngster at Bonwire spends Saturdays weaving kente-cloth.

    g) Nana Akwasi Gyamfi kentehene busy at work.

    h) Machine-woven kente.

    i) Machine-print kente

Picture # 2

    a) Nana Akwasi Gyamfi in action weaving **Mampam-se** Kente pattern: predominant colors are black & white.

    b) A twenty-year old man is seen weaving **Adjwini-asa**

    c) An elderly man is seen sewing together **ntoma-ban** finished kente strips.

    d) An 8 yr old boy going through nurturing process in the kente-weaving village. He is seen weaving **Asase-ntoma.**

    e) A warp stretches from the loom front to about 8 to 12 feet. It is fastened on a rock and secured by wooden rod.

Picture # 3

a) An assortment of some classic kente patterns; from top, **sika futro,** ordinary-woven black & white cloth, **oyoko-mma, emma-da,** (not known), **adjwini-asa, abusua-ye-dom, ahwepan** (ordinary woven cloth), **mampam-se.**

b) A modern factory in Ghana that produces machine-woven-kente

c) Kente merchants and merchandise in the village and in the cities

Picture # 4

Osagyefo Dr. Kwame Nkrumah (1909-1972)
First President Republic of Ghana (1957-66)
draped in **Mmogya bi ye dom** kente.

Picture # 5

Typical Ashantis in their kente cloths.

a) Opanin Kofi Darkwah in his Abusua-ye-dom kente

b) Mame Adjoa Nyame in her Oyoko-mma kente over wax-print. Her entire outfit is called **dansi-nkran**

c) Kentehene Nana Akwasi Gyamfi in one-of-a-kind Abrimpon-ntoma kente

d) Opanin Darkwah in a nwen-ntoma (ordinary woven cloth)

e) Mr Asamoah-Yaw and family in Sika-futro kente during his son's graduation ceremony.

KENTE CLOTH
Introduction to History

By Ernest Asamoah-Yaw

First Publication 1992 NY.
Second Publication 1994 Ghana .
Third Publication (revised) 1999 NY

Copyright (c) 1992
ISBN 0-9635566-0-6

DEDICATION

This is dedicated to all those who helped to make this work possible. I am particularly thankful to the following individuals whose contribution formed the bases of the book; Nana Kwasi Gyamfi-Kentehene, Solo and brother, and all those who participated in the interview during my trips to Bonwire.

Even though it is impossible to quantify her enormous support to the entire project right from the beginning to the finish, it would be inappropriate if I don't mention my dearest wife's name Mrs. Juliana Asamoah-Yaw. If this work is worth anything at all, she is the one person that ought to be congratulated. Mr George Antwi, Nana Osei Kwame, Kwa-Apiagyei, Lou Black, Dr. Badoe, and many more who patiently and critically read over the work and corrected many of my mistakes, I wish I could say more than thank you. Ante Afua Agyeman did the initial typing work. My son Kwaku Badoe Asamoah should be mentioned for his research in the libraries, plus my little daughter Afua Brago Asamoah's persistent questioning about the book "when are we finishing the book?", a question she asked many times everyday for two years never stopped ringing in my ears. I also like to thank all those who encouraged me by asking questions about kente cloth and Afrikan fabrics in general and the many hundreds of customers who visited our store. It was these very people who inspired me to probe into this field of study. My bank manager Mr. John Scott and staff assisted in several hidden ways only known to my family. Dr. Deas's remarks finalized the work. Thank you once again to all kente cloth admirers, it is you who made this possible.

CONTENTS

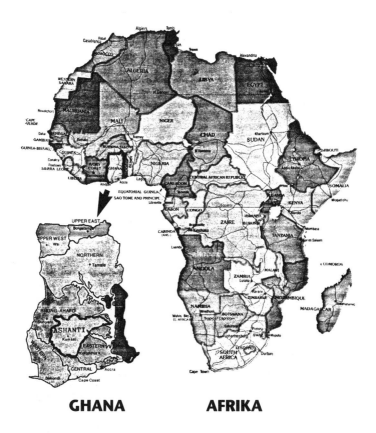

GHANA   **AFRIKA**

Map of Afrika, Ghana, and Ashanti Region

INTRODUCTION

Among modern Kente weavers, there appears to be only a small fraction who can claim to have adequate historical knowledge of this ancient fabric. The fact is that there exists no single comprehensive document anywhere which addresses clearly such issues as its definition, its origin, creators of the classic patterns, color combination of the traditional designs, its usage in the olden days and its application to our contemporary world. Such possible new notions as Kente Ideology and its composite myths plus the international significance of the cloth undoubtedly require research. This work is merely an attempt to clear some of the doubts about the cloth. The book is not intended to be a panacea of every kente question. It is only a prelude to a better understanding of the cloth. Its admirers are unquestionably anxious to know something more than its glittering facade behind which hides the true essence of Ashanti culture.

Chapter One
KENTE CLOTH

Description

According to **Nana Akwasi Gyamfi of Bonwire** (the king of all kente weavers in Ashanti region), and the most authoritative person in the kente weaving industry in Ghana, the word kente represents what he calls *Adwini-nweni-ntoma.* This can be translated literally as *creative, thoughtful,* or *designer's-woven-cloth.* In Twi dialect (the language of Ashanti people), the word **kɛnte** or kente rhymes with two other words, namely; **kɛtɛ** (pronounced as kerter) and **kɛntɛn** (pronounced as kerntern). Kɛnte (pronounced as kernty), spelled currently as kente is a woven cloth.

1

Kɛtɛ is a woven mat and kɛntɛn is a woven basket. All the three words have one thing in common. They are woven in the same interlock technique. The difference is that Kɛnte is woven with a fine yarn or thread, while kɛtɛ and kɛntɛn are both woven with natural fiber from palm tree branches or cane fibre. Kɛtɛ, Kɛntɛn and Kɛnte weaving process in Ashanti are very ancient. They were created out of basic human need for comfort and leisure. Kente cloth weaving process is not much different from weaving any other cloth. The basic principles are the same. It involves turning and twisting yarns in order to separate individual strands and organizing the individual yarns into their color groupings, then, depending on the choice of pattern, lining them up linearly into a loom to form the warp process or horizontal shapes. This is followed by the weft process, which consists of carefully spinning the yarn on the bobbin to be used for interlacing or throwing across the warp from left to right and right to left, followed by a series of woofing; that is pressing the lines of thread tightly against each other. Pictogram blocks or shapes or images in the cloth are created by picking very carefully some warp threads and throwing a series of wefts in several sequences until the pattern is created.

There exists no complete written history of kente cloth anywhere, and for this reason our knowledge of the cloth is based on elder weavers' dexterity and recollection of the past as handed down by word of mouth from generation to generation. The following therefore, is only a brief history of kente cloth as narrated by Kentehene (Kente Chief) Nana Akwasi Gyamfi of Bonwire-Ashanti region Ghana. Nana Gyamfi is sixty-three years old at the time of this interview. He started weaving kente cloth since the age of three and has been recognized and enstooled for the past seventeen years by Nana Asantehene (the King of Asante) as the kente chief. This title makes him the most knowledgeable person in the field of kente cloth weaving. Kente cloth is an Ashanti traditional cloth. A genuine kente is hand woven in a wooden loom to the size of approximately four and a half inches by one-hundred and forty-four inches ($4^1/_2$ x 144) per long strip. It consists of two or more color combination and woven in geometric or pictogram shapes. Asante people of Ashanti region in Ghana created the cloth originally for their leaders to wear on special occasions. At first, the cloth was woven in black and white cotton yarn and with simple designs called **Ahwepan.** Raw cotton and dye products were locally available and it was later on in the years when weavers were able to dye other colorful threads by the use of plants. For example, **Dubuma** tree provided black fluid for black color; **Dua-sika** tree fluid made gold or yellow color available; **Kasie**-tree for red color. In some cases, the colors were tapped from back of trees, while in others the bark had to be peeled off the tree and boiled or processed before top quality fast color could be produced to bleach cotton yarns. It is true also to say that fruits and roots provided another source of coloring materials. Colorful kente gained popularity much faster than the black and white as a result of persistent quest for exclusive quality cloth among the chiefs. Black and white kente is still made in Bonwire yet its importance has diminished and given way to bright colorful combinations of gold, red, blue, and green cloth. In their attempt to let the black and white (ahwepan) kente co-exist with the colorful ones, the weavers frequently create new patterns in black and white and assign names and significance to them. For example there is a black and white kente called

Nanka-tiri or **Mampam-see** for articulate and often despised personalities.

Myths About Kente Cloth Origin
Spider-Web Paradox

The most popular legend about the cloth is the SPIDER-WEB MYTH. All kente weavers at the village of **Bonwire** including Nana Akwasi Gyamfi (Kente Chief), do believe that their knowledge of kente weaving could be traced from two hunters namely: **Nana Koragu** and **Nana Ameyaw.** Once upon a time these two hunters went to the forest to hunt for animals. While searching for a prey, they saw a spider on a tree weaving a spider-web. They became very curious about the skill with which the insect was turning and twisting a self-produced silky thread from below its abdomen to weave the web. Each of the spider's eight fingers/legs performed a different function of the intricate pattern that had never been seen before. The hunters returned home so amused that they started building structures and tools with which they immitated the spider's weaving process and its graphical inlays to create the cloth which later on became known as kente-cloth.

A Discussion of the Spider Web Paradox

It is a common knowledge in Ashanti that bush hunting takes place only in the night and never in the day time. Hunters believe that animals can be surprised, become confused, and motionless when they see their glaring light in the night. It is also true in the tropics that animals hunt for food in the night than in the day time.

Again some experts claim that most animals would react and possibly feel threatened and therefore run away when they see an unusual bright light approaching. The spider would not be an exception to these observations. Also considering the size of a spider, a man would have to go very close to be able to see properly the skills of this ingeneous creature in action; most likely conclusion here is that the spider would stop weaving and probably hide itself from the hunters sight. It is not likely that the spider would have the courage to continue weaving under the watchful eyes of the hunters. For this myth be true, one would have to assume a few things: *firstly* that the two hunters (Nana Koragu and Nana Ameyaw) must have gone to the bush in the night to hunt and could not have seen the spider busy at work weaving, but rather possibly saw the spider's web on a tree and went to the site again during day time to observe the structures of the web or, *secondly* that the two brothers actually did see a spider weaving a web on a tree in day time during one of their errands to the bush or, *thirdly* that the two brothers were master weavers already who carefully studied the artistry of the spider and incorporated the graphics of its web into their normal loom-weaving process in an attempt to create a different cloth which later on became known as kente cloth. As already explained else where, the basic difference between Kente cloth and other woven cloth is that kente contains defined graphics while the others are plain and only horizentally structured, normally called *nwen-ntoma* as opposed to *kente-nwen-toma.*

It is further explained by Nana Akwasi Gyamfi that even though Nana Kragu and Nana Ameyaw created or invented kente cloth, **it was** *Nana Otaa Kraban* **who improved upon their invention. He was the first person to weave kente cloth and gave it a name OYOKOMMAN or OYOKOMMA** (pronounced as oryuko-mann or oryuko-mmar). It was he who gave significance to the cloth and introduced it to the Ashanti royal family.

It is a tradition in Ashanti that the person

that sits (not literally) on the Golden Stool (Asantehene) or the King of Ashanti must be a true member of the oyoko clan **(oyoko nnton).** Oyoko is one of the seven principal clans in Ashanti. The other six are *Aduana, Bretuo, Asona, Ekoana, Aseneye,* and *Asakyeri.* Knowing very well the supremacy of oyoko clan, Nana Otaa Kraban designed this cloth and named it oyoko-mman (oyoko-state) or oyoko-mma (oyoko-kinship) and presented it to *Okatakyie-Otumfuo-Nana Asantehene* the most powerful king of Ashanti region. Because of the luxurious and exclusive nature of the cloth, the King created a stool or an institution in the name of the weaver; hence the title *Nana* comes before Otaa Kraban's name, symbolizing a new enstoolment in the village of Bonwire. The present Kente chief confirms that Nana Otaa Kraban's stool is still inherited by his kith and kin in the village.

Kente as an Invention of the Moshie Tribe

In absence of written history or recorded evidence, there is always enough room for speculation and misinterpretation. Most of the weavers interviewed at Bonwire and elsewhere have heard of a story that an Ashanti King travelled to the northern region of Ghana to meet the *Moshie* Chief who was dressed in a magnificient woven cloth. He was so fascinated about it and asked if he could travel to Ashanti region with the weaver to weave the same cloth for him. The weaver was permitted to travel to Ashanti region with the king to be the King's weaver. It is believed that the weaver settled at Bonwire and taught the village people how to weave cloth. There is no evidence in the village of where the weaver might have settled nor is there a recollection of any single weaver whose ancestor learnt his trade from a Moshie weaver. If there was such a weaver at all, he never settled there. One thing that is known among all Ghanaians is the fact that the Moshie people, like many other tribes in the upper regions or the immediate southern part of the Sahara, have their own kinds of traditional woven cloth. The Ashantis call them **fugu;** and when made into a dress it is known as **batakari** for the top and togas for the pants. Fugu somehow became part of the Ashanti military outfit during the latter part of the 19th century. War leaders dressed in fugu smocks with coloful talisman decorations were considered spiritually powerful and invincible. Even in modern times, some Ashanti chiefs put on these outfits when attending the funeral of a paramont chief. Fugu and kente cloth have few things in common. Both are woven in strips in wooden frames with colorful threads. Their differences are many. Fugu is very seldom woven in horizontal and vertical patterns simultaneously.

It contains no short-spaced graphics or geometrics. Its closest resemblance is the ordinary woven-cloth nwentoma of the Ashantis, but even here, the Ashantis emphasize on using fine threads as opposed to the wooly unrefined yarns preferred by the moshie weavers. These two products are from two distinct traditional groups and must not be taken as an immitation of each other. Each one must be considered as superior in its own culture.

Kente as an Invention of the Ewe Tribe

There is a consistent consensus in Ghana and elsewhere that Kente cloth originated from Ashanti region of Ghana. Among Ghanaians, kente belongs to Asante people in the same way as one sees the tartan or the kilt for the Scottish, sari for India, kimono for the Japanese, fugu for the Moshie, mud-cloth for Mali and so forth. Recent inquiries about history of kente appear to indicate that the cloth probably originated from the Volta region of Ghana. A few people even go to the extent of claiming that the Ewes taught the Ashantis how to weave. A common thing among these critics is that none has any supporting proof. Historically, there is enough cultural evidence to demonstrate that kente cloth couldn't have come from any part of the world other than Ashanti region. Until the invention of modern machines, every ethnic group throughout the world (including those in Europe, Asia, America, and Afrika) depended on such clothing as those woven by hand and looms or animals-skins clothing, processed fiber clothing, and processed wood-barks clothing. Both Ewes and Ashantis of Ghana passed through this fashion evolution. The Ewes had their own kind of woven cloth, and the Ashantis too had theirs. Both groups used wooden looms. Both weave narrow strips before joining them to form large blanket-size cloth. Also there is no doubt that the two groups had some similarities in the equipment and the methods of weaving cloth. But so do the ethnic groups in Nigeria, Zaire, Burkina Faso, Chad and a few others. as already documented by Picton & Mack book called the African Textiles. The finished fabrics and the manufacturing methods of the traditional weavers in the above Afrikan countries are almost but not exactly the same. Each one is different in its own peculiar way. And it will therefore be a gross mistake to draw simple conclusions that bacause they are almost alike, one group must have copied from the other. Even though the allegation may have a substance, we must not distort the known traditional facts until there is a conclusive evidence to sustantiate the claim.

A close observation of the two fabrics indicate that there exists a vast structural difference between them. For example, the patterns are different, color emphasis in each design is different, and more especially their styles are quite distinct from each other. Ewe weavers traditionally tend to create images of natural objects such as animals, human artifacts and caricatures. Goba Tange family of weavers is a classic example of weavers from the Volta region. This family traces its weaving history far beyond the 19th century, and they are exceptionally good at weaving images into narrow strip fabrics. In fact they try to display their creativity during the weaving process and can actually portray anything including numbers, figures, and symbols in their fabrics. But being an expert in onething does not necessarily make one a master in everything or something that another ethnic group is known to have created and specialized, as is indeed narrowly percieved by these critics. A significant point to note also is that consistency of patterns is not common among the Ewe traditional clothing. A typical size of a strip is about two to three inches wide and more similar to that of the Yoruba's **aso-oke.** Single-thread as opposed to double-thread weaving is the norm. Ashanti weavers on the other hand maintain approximately four-inch width for both single and double-thread. A major difference which must be noted also is that Ashanti kente has always been consistent with abstract designs and to everyone pattern they assign a name or significance. And it is because of this repetitive nature of their style that continuity of the popularly known kente patterns today have been in existence for the longest time. These patterns have always been referred to by their Ashanti names from time immemorial.

The recent expansion of demand and supply of kente has generated more curiosity in everything concerning the cloth at home and abroad.

Consequently, weaving has become a very lucrative profession. Weavers of other traditional fabrics in Afrika who are familiar with working with looms that produce narrow strips are vigorously changing their skills to copy kente patterns. Ivory Coast, Togoland, and Senegal are known to be producing the genuine kente in commercial quantities for the American market. In Ghana, needless-to-say, kente trade is one of the fastest growing business. It is not just the Ewes who are copying Asante kente *(woven cloth with abstract and traditionally meaningful designs)* but also weavers in other regions are seriously getting involved. It is hoped that this wide spread interest in the cloth will stimulate more research that may prevent permanently such unnecessary debate relating to its origins.

Chapter Two
APPRENTICESHIP & TRAINING OF KENTE WEAVER

There is no single academic institution at any level (from elementary to University) in Ghana that specializes in kente-weaving or trains people to become *professional* kente-weavers. The industry itself is still domestic in every sense of the word. The looms and all equipments are owned by the individual weavers themselves. He either builds them himself or that he inherits them from his uncle or father. All the stages of production are undertaken by the same person from start to finish. In the villages, over 90% of all weavers are wholesalers as well as retailers of their own products. At Bonwire for example, most males over the age of 35 years possess their own equipments for weaving cloth. Kente cloth is produced in the homes or backyards of individuals. They are not made in factories with complex industrial machines and computers. No division of labour nor specialization. A weaver must therefore be a master of all the functions involved in the industry including building his own loom, tools, equipments; knowing where and how to obtain raw materials; knowing how to process yarns and set them up in the loom; and finally starts to demonstrate his acquired weaving skills which he has learned through a growth process in the family from childhood to manhood. Production and distribution of kente cloth has always been a home affair, a family entity and a personal business. Training to become a weaver has also always remain a domestic affair. A weaver learns his trade through the traditional nurturing process in the family. As a child growing up in the village, it is part of your daily routine to assist elder family members in cleaning, washing, farming, weaving etc. etc. It is part of the general cultural education that males in particular pass through to manhood. Thus a weaver's son who may later train through a college or university to become an accountant for example could easily sit in a loom and demonstrates the art he learned when he was growing up in the village. It should be noted here that weaving is essentially a male profession in Ashanti. There are, off-course, a few exceptions where a female can weave as well as a male. Even though she might not make it her profession, she could still weave the most complex patterns simply because she had the exposure at home. Five year-olds start with what they call **Asaase-ntoma;** where a child sits on the ground close to papa or uncle with the two legs stretched forward: he ties one big toe with one end of a long string, the other end goes up around his waist-line to be fastened to the other toe. He picks another color shorter thread and ties it to the center of one line on the toes and starts throwing it from left to right and right to left rapidly up and down the two stretched toe lines until the fabric takes shape. This process goes on for days and weeks under adult supervision. The child learns at this stage all the body movements involved in weaving *(see picture 2d in illustration).* Until recently, before the early 1960s, weaving in general was a part-time business. Most weavers were farmers and still are. A few are traders and only a fraction are full-time weavers. Most weavers that live in and around Bonwire and Wonoo villages have had formal education and are able to read and write. This is common among the youth. Most of the elderly weavers who can articulate well on kente cloth are over the age of sixty and illiterate. Kentehene Nana Akwasi Gyamfi, for example, had no formal education, but he understands the fundamentals of english and arithmetic. Like many of his peers, he learned his trade from his parents and became a master by constant practice and dedication. By the age of fifteen, a village youngster is able to weave most of the less complex patterns; it is only the experienced person who can weave such designs as Adwini-asa and Oyokomma. It is also believed that some patterns can not be copied because of their complexities, unless its originator is present. A classic example is a pattern called *"Asesia"* which was woven by a famous weaver from the village and presented to Asantehene. The weaver died about twenty years ago and it will take a genius to duplicate it. And according to kente chief, Nana Asantehene is believed to have the largest collection of the most beautiful, complex and the rarest kentes in the world.

Recent Changes in Training the Youth to Become Kente Weavers

Increased demand for the cloth at home and expansion of demand from abroad have created a shortage in supply of kente. Consequently, some elementary and vocational schools have employed professional weavers to visit their schools to teach children how to weave the cloth. A few successful businessmen and experienced weavers have organized some young ones into business units to be able to increase output and also train them to become proficient in every aspect of the profession. It is interesting to note that it takes approximately three to five years to train a beginner on a full-time bases to become a competent kente weaver. Again, an experienced weaver will use about four hours to weave a simple plain strip kente-cloth of about (4x72) inches with single thread. While it will take the same weaver more than eight hours (depending on his experience) to make Adwini-asa kente strip of the same size at one sitting without a break.

Chapter Three
HOW AND WHEN KENTE CLOTH IS USED

Before kente there was the ordinary woven cloth as already explained else where. Ideally, kente cloth was developed as a luxury or a special cloth for special people and for special occasions. A classic equivalent in the western tradition is the tuxedo. An Englishman or a Yankee, for example, dressed in black tuxedo is presumed to be attending a wedding or a banquet. A tuxedo was probably not created for this purpose but this is how it is generally used. Kente cloth is known to have been created with a purpose and thus it is purposefully used. A person dressed in kente cloth in Ashanti is always seen as having a special purpose in mind. Its original creators designed each pattern with a vision that the cloth will carry a specific message of its user whenever and wherever it is used. The intentions of the master designers were to create an exclusively beautiful cloth that will tell its audience the wearer's mission at the time, his character, his mood, social status and etc. This is so because all Ashanti traditional kente patterns do carry traditional names and significance. There is no exception to this custom. For this reason, there is a paramount chief's cloth *(abrempong-ntoma)* for every festive occasion and durbars. Ashanti statesmen in the past were known to be dressed in kente cloth whenever they met foreign dignitaries. They were also known to have a habit of ordering specially created kente design whenever there was a traditional ceremony that required their presence. It is true also to say that there is an ancient tradition which demands that nobody wears in a public place the same cloth that a king may wear. A royal kente may be worn only once a year or once in the kings lifetime when on the throne, because His Majesty is expected by his subjects to be in a magnificent outfit every time they see him in public. And for this reason, kings and chiefs were rarely seen in public places. They accepted invitations only when it was stately important or traditionally necessary to do so. It is a common knowledge in Ashanti that kings or chiefs have the largest collection of kente in the royal depository. The Asantehene's kente depository is called ***Sesia-adaka.*** This is where all the rarest patterns are preserved. Whenever a new cloth is needed Kentehene and his best weavers at Bonwire would be summoned to **Kumasi-Manhyia** (official residence of **Otumfuo Nana Asantehene**) palace to choose from two to four patterns from which they would pick and fuse designs to generate a new pattern, and give it a name and significance; or they may decide to create something completely new to be-fit the Royal Highness' impending occasion. Kente cloth as a product for the kings only, gradually, changed and absorbed into its usage the entire members of the aristocracy. This necessitated growth in creation of new patterns for the prince and princess, nephews and uncles, queen-mothers and kins plus the entire patrician class of Ashanti kingdom. *Kyemea* kente pattern for example was created for queenmothers. By the turn of the 19th century, the British imperial powers had neutralized the Ashantis and imposed their system of government on them. Nevertheless, it co-existed with the indigenous traditions. This required formation of academic institutions to train local people to administer the colony. A new bourgeois class of local inhab-itants with authority to administer the enlarged

Gold Coast colony (including Ashanti Kingdom) had been born. Their tastes for excellence and beauty were not different from the traditional rulers and the foreign masters. Kente weavers did not waste time in creating new patterns to commemorate the changing events. From this period on silk scarfs had been introduced by the European merchants to the African market. While the women use them as head-wraps, weavers dismantled the fabric and reused the silk-threads to weave kente-cloth traditionally called **sirikye-kente.** Thus before the First World War, kente was available not only in fine cotton but also in silk and rayon or a combination of both threads obtained from China and India through European trade.

Chapter Four
LEGENDS ABOUT KENTE CLOTH

ADJWINI-ASA: One of the famous Ashanti traditional kente can properly be described as End of design, Ultimate design, a product of an exhausted effort to create *the best* design. One can simply call it the best design by definition. In Akan language, *adjwini* means brains, thought, idea, or design; *asa* means finished, completed, ended, or accomplished. The two words combined literally means end of a design or a product of an ingenious artist. According to legend, a weaver was chosen by a king to weave the best kente the world had ever known. The weaver used all his expertise to fuse all the known designs and extracted the best in them to create a unique pattern for the king. It is believed that in the olden days, whenever there was a plan for the king to attend to a special function there was always a plan to get the king a new kente cloth. That it was the elders or the kingmakers and especially the queenmother who chose what cloth *nana* would wear in all official occasions. It is a fact however that some traditional leaders still maintain this tradition. The king may consult his closest confidant or the queenmother or an elderstatesman about his final choice of cloth for the day. The emphasis these days is on new symbolic cloth for the occasion and not necessarily Adjwini Asa kente. When selection for the weaver is finally completed, The weaver would proudly accept the royal order, for it was the greatest honor to be chosen to weave for the king. Because of the design's complexities, no time was set for the completion of the work. His royal highness was also aware of the unique custom that went with weaving this particular cloth. For this and other reasons, the weaver was permitted to take as much time as necessary to finish the product. It could take him one month, one year, ten years or more to weave the best for the best. A typical man-size kente-cloth is about eight feet by twelve feet, when the narrow strips are sewn together in the form of a large blanket or bed-sheet. On the presentation day, there would be the weaver and his next-of-kin, the elders who chose the weaver, and possibly the king himself at the royal palace. According to this legend, the next-of-kin would have to be present because the weaver could be executed if the king made such a pronouncement. This was believed to be the custom, because if the weaver was allowed to live he might duplicate the same design for another king or some other individuals. According to Ashanti tradition, the king's outfit must be different from all others at all social gatherings. It must be exclusively rich-looking, very attractive, and most beautiful cloth among all others. Nobody was expected to wear the exact cloth as that of the king on the same occasion. This ancient tradition is still observed even among the petty-chiefs. It is understandable, therefore that some weavers knowing very well the consequences of finishing and delivering the cloth, took their time to weave it. It was like preparing under duress ones own death warrant with his chosen time for an honorable and dignified death. There are some stories that sometimes the king never lived to see the finished product. The king or the weaver or both might have died before the cloth was completed. While the weaver's next-of-kin was not traditionally obliged to continue the royal order, he was entitled to inherit all the deceased property.

In case the weaver decided to finish and present the cloth to the king, he would be honored such that his name would live forever as the best kente weaver who sacrificed his life to weave the best for the best. The king's pronouncement for the execution would have to be preceded by an earlier investigation proving that the weaver could not be trusted to live without weaving the same cloth for another person. A stool would be created in his name. This process was synonymous with the establishment of a new institution in the area. Thus the weaver may have died, but his successor would reign in his name. Some traditional weavers believe that since most weavers then were aged and knew the rest of their lives were very short, a few of them preferred to pass away with grace. It must be noted here that a premature death of the king did not automatically stop the weaving process. the work would have to continue regardless, because the finished kente would belong to the stool or the royalty and not necessarily the king per se`. On the other hand, a weaver who successfully delivered the cloth could be rewarded with **abodin** a title, honor, or a commendation. This could be any one or two of the following; **oke-sei** the great, **opanin** elder, **obadwinba** a thinker or intellectual, *nana* excellency, **onwen-ima-ohene** the kings' weaver, and **kentehene** kente-chief etc., etc., These credentials uplifted ordinary citizens into statesmen and role models. Descendants of great weavers aspired to become as good as their fathers and uncles who wove or created special kente pattern for the king. This may be a fable story but it is possibly through these inspirations that kente cloth industry grew and maintained its present status throughout the years.

ABUSUA-YE-DOM: This is a protest cloth according to legend. It was often used as mediators cloth. Kingmakers in Ashanti are the elders of the state. They are responsible for appointing new kings or traditional leaders. They are also responsible for removing them from throne. It may consist of local people who can articulate on local customs and culture. They do not necessarily belong to the same clan as that of the ruling chief. When elders meet in state to remove a stubborn chief, all those in favour of the motion would appear in this kind of kente at the meeting. This is usually preceded by a cordial approach and diplomacy to normalize state affairs. When communication breaks down then the elders resorts to silent means to show their persistent disapproval of running traditional affairs by wearing abusua-ye-dom kente, signifying their desire to replace the leadership. This could be just a single person's protest or that of many. The kingmakers ways of demonstrating a desire to replace the existing leader varied from district to district. For example in **Kumawu,** a town in the north-eastern part of Ashanti region, the hard-core traditional king-makers have a peculiar way of voicing out their desire to replace a chief. All those who support-ed de-stoolment would refuse to shave their mustaches and beards as long as the existing chief remained enstooled. Everybody becomes clean-shaven on the very day the chief abdicates or is removed from the throne. It was particu-larly important in the olden days in some Ashanti villages that elders voiced opinions by way of dresses than any other means. It was appearances not actions that spoke louder than words. It is still true in modern day Ashanti.

Other Examples:

OYOKO-MA OR OYOKO-MMAN Pro-nounced as *"or-yu-ko-mma"*. This is defined as the "children or kins of oyoko clan", the heirs of

Ashanti Monarchy or custodians of the Ashanti Golden Stool — the highest seat of power of the Ashanti kingdom. This is one of the oldest patterns designed for the king and kins of the dynasty to *distinguish* themselves from the rest. Its modified form was later on created for the commoners.

EMMAA DA Pronounced as *"ermar-da"*. This can be defined as *first of its kind* or that which has never been seen or occurred. This was designed for the aristocratic class to show its *pomposity*.

EPEPIAKYIRE OR EPIAKYIRE Pronounced as *"erpeer-chry"*. A fortress, a barrier, a barricade or a fence. This was purposely designed for leaders of the Ashanti kingdom. It signifies their *invincibility*.

SIKA FUTRO Pronounced as *"ce-ka foot-ro"*. This is translated as gold powder or *gold-dust*.

This pattern was conceived with *affluence* or wealth in mind. The design speaks for itself that the wearer is rich in everything. His *wealth* is as *plentiful* as *dust.*

KYEMIA Pronounced as *"che-me-a"*. This was designed for Asantehenmma (the queen of queens in Ashanti). And later on became a kente *cloth for ladies in the royal family.* This is to indicate who is who among the ladies in kingdom.

ETI KRO NKO AGYINA Pronounced as *"erty-kro-nkor-adj-e-nar"*. This means it takes more than one head to form a committee or to take a good decision. The designer of this classic kente intended to create an exclusive cloth that could be worn by a member or members who may disagree or refuse to accept the consensus of decision makers. It was purposefully designed to be worn to protest wisely with dignity.

FATHIA FATA NKRUMAH Pronounced as *"Fa-tia fa-ter Nk-ru-mar"*. Literally this means "it is befitting to have Miss Fathia as Dr. Kwame Nkrumah's wife". There was a public outcry about the leader's choice of spouse from Egypt instead of Ghana. He disregarded public opinion and in December 1957 he married an Egyptian lady called Fathia Halen Ratzk. In memory of this historic event, a Kente weaver designed a pattern and named it as such.

NOTE *The above are only a few of the most popular classic kente patterns. Refer to picture 3a.*

Chapter Five
OTHER FORMS OF KENTE CLOTH

A cloth or an artwork can be called kente imitation, if it has the look of any of the traditional hand-loom-woven kente patterns. For this reason, we can conveniently say the cloth comes in three different forms. First, there is the genuine Ashanti hand-loom-woven kente. Secondly, the Broadloom Machine-woven kente, and thirdly, the Machine-print kente.

Machine-Print Kente

This is a fabric or a cloth (gray goods) that has been processed to look like a kente pattern. If a specific pattern is engraved on a copper roller or drum to print the image of kente, the material can properly be called kente imitation. These are mass-produced on conveyor belts and available in twelve yards bundles by forty-five inches wide. It is the most affordable among all the kente materials. It must be emphasized however that these materials are mere copies and do not have meanings to them. They should be taken only by their face value. There are as many kente-print patterns as there are in the genuine hand-woven. It is not possible to obtain the exact printed copy of a real authentic loom-woven kente, but few of them however do come close. The first kente print is believed to have been made in Holland by a company called Vlisco. This is the oldest known and pioneer company that still produces the best quality African cotton wax prints. Even though it is the world leader in the industry, an Ivory Coast based company (Gonfreville ERG) is the leading manufacturer of imitation kente today. Vlisco specializes in printing the real dutch wax and its derivatives for specific indigenous Afrikan markets. The following countries print some of the traditional patterns (often copied from Vlisco) in small quantities; Senegal, Zambia, Nigeria, Pakistan and Ghana.

Machine-Woven Kente

This material is completely different from the print and the authentic hand-woven ones, and they must not be confused with each other. The patterns are created during the weaving process in the same way as the hand-weave method by modern industrial broad-loom machines. The finished fabric looks and feels different. The texture is almost identical to the hand woven kente. Both are heavy and rough by touch and appearance. They are basically horizontal patterns with sequential blocks of vertical graphics. This is less expensive compared to the original hand woven kente. They are available in bundles of 20 yards or more by 56 inches wide in multi-colored shades. Ghana is the first country to introduce machine-woven kente in commercial quantities. The company that made the first attempt to use modern machines to weave kente is called SPINTEX. It is based in Ghana and it is still the only known company that manufactures the fabric. It is important to know that machine woven kente has no traditional significance and even though some of the patterns have traditional Afrikan symbols such as the Ashanti stool and the Egyptian Ankh, they do not serve any particular purpose. They are complimentary to the real cloth. Both machine-weave and machine-print should not be considered as substitute to each other, nor to the hand woven cloth. They do not carry the same traditional historical substance that is inherent with the real Ashanti hand-loom kente. The producers of these imitations did not plan to create a cloth to replace the original. They simply attempted to mass-produce a cloth that looks real and possibly serve the same purpose at a lower price. By this token, they succeeded and should be congratulated. *Refer to pictures 1h and 1i.*

Chapter Six
KENTE CLOTH
JOURNEY TO AMERICA
INTERNAL & EXTERNAL FACTORS

Internal Factors (Population Diversities & Search for Identity)

These are the ingredients that exist within the continent of America (north, central, and south) not just United States of America, which can be assessed as contributory factors responsible for bringing kente cloth to the country. The first on the list is the histories of the countries and their multi-racial compositions; secondly, the philosophy of slavery prior to the early 1950s; thirdly, the inevitable human need for a cultural identity.

Historically speaking, all American countries with the exception of a few small Islands were founded by people from all over the world including Afrika. United States is the only country outside Afrika with the highest population of black people, currently 29.9 million and over 12% of the entire population. It is more than one and a half times the size of Ghana with 16 million people. This is the first largest ethnic group in modern history that were forbidden any knowledge of their culture for more than a century and subsequently forced to adopt foreign cultures which had no clear resemblance to their natural Afrikan habitat. The ancient philosophy of using black people as chattels persisted even during the emancipation movement of the last century to the middle of this century, The primary cause of black people's agitation was highly linked to his lost of cultural identity. The natural quality or trait without which he is half human, was taken away from him and created a vacuum. The vacuum was never filled and never could have been filled with anything other than that which was truly his "the Afrikan culture". In this sense, today's adaptation of kente cloth by Afrikan-Americans is only the beginning of social revolution that can not be stopped.

The trend will go on until those to be born in future can proudly and truthfully, physically and spiritually honor themselves with the goodies of the motherland. This can be termed as **the iron law of culture and identity;** *(take away one's culture you have taken away his identity. No matter how much you try to replace it, there will come a time when the original culture will prevail)*. Kente cloth is a mere beginning. Its users today will inevitably graduate tomorrow to adopt Afrikan religions, Afrikan family life style, Afrikan names and languages, Afrikan foods etc., etc.

The 1950's marked a new beginning of political awareness among black people all over the world. Before this period, expression of ones political views was mainly an intellectual exercise. It was only a few who could articulate properly the causes and effects of local and international sensitive issues. The accepted mode of demonstrating ones approval or disapproval of economic and social problems was either through the pen or the barrel of a gun. It was not a coincidence therefore that the blackman chose both. The master was in control of both the gun, pen and money. He decided what was lawful and what was unlawful. Even though the pen was mightier than the sword as a tool for causing changes or addressing the blackman's needs universally, there was something lacking and still wanting in certain quarters that was needed to enhance his humanity. This was his identity, his name, his culture, his id, and that natural Afrikan habitat from which he was spirited away for centuries. This hypocritical master was definitely aware of Afrikan cultural beauty and its intellect, but out of sheer wickedness, he preferred not to talk about it because it might alter the historic master/servant relationship; so naive was he however, that he could not foresee that everything that has a beginning has an end, and that someday the truth will come out. Black leadership in America and Africa had to find a way to erase the public image or perception of Afrika and to replace that with the truth. That Afrika should not be seen as a continent with monkies and naked people roaming in forests, the Tarzan image mentality, but rather one with a different civilization, different culture and different value systems. That the people of Afrikan descent must be informed that Afrika has a lot to be proud of. The new generation of black leaders saw radicalism as the first step to regenerate the long lost self-esteem and pride among black people. They went beyond 'Garvyism'. (Marcus Garvey's gospel of the inter-war period that all Afrikan-Americans must return to Afrika for two reasons; 1) It is their natural habitat, 2) the master did not want to live with him as a human being and on equal bases. This notion was modified after the second world war by the new breed of black leaders. They maintained that all Afrikan-Americans need not go back to Afrika to settle, because their mothers and fathers significantly contributed to build America from scratch. Blacks can continue to live in America to be able to reap the maximum benefits of their forefathers' sacrifices. They must nevertheless seek at all times to claim back the lost Afrikan heritage. There should be no shame in changing from a borrowed culture to one that is naturally yours. It is not shameful to learn an Afrikan language, or change your name for an Afrikan name, or eat an Afrikan food, or wear an Afrikan cloth or neck-tie to work. To detest any of these, is to be shameful of your very nature. How can a blackman measure his excellence fully within a culture that is imposed on him. The early black-leaders were surely radicals. They identified themselves completely with the motherland and rejected the conventional ways and methods of solving problems. They talked and dressed differently. Malcolm *Little* deleted his last name and replaced it temporally with an 'X' pending such a time when he would discover his true identity. Elijah *Poole* (Minister, Muslim leader and civil rights activist) changed his last name to Elijah Muhammad. *Francis* **N**krumah of Ghana (human rights leader, reformer and president of First Republic Ghana) *re-*changed his first name to Kwame. The list can go on and on. Nkrumah for example, toured all over Ghana and Afrika several occasions dressed in either kente-cloth or fugu. He appeared overseas many times in international conferences such as the United Nations, Organization of Afrikan Unity, and the British Commonwealth dressed in kente cloth draped around his body as it is traditionally worn in Ghana. Again in the late 1950s, during one of his official visits to the USA to negotiate with Kaiser Industries to build the Akosombo Dam in Ghana, Mr. Gbedema (a prominent Nkrumah's minister) had on a magnificent kente cloth symbolizing his pride in our culture. Nana Kwame Gyebi Ababio, ex-Omanhene (paramount chief) of Essumja Traditional area has recorded that in 1948 when King George V of England invited the Gold Coast Traditional Chiefs (including himself as Ashanti representative) to discuss Gold Coast Independence issue in London, he wore kente cloth to show his pride in Ashanti tradition. And apart from the chiefs from northern territories who had Fugu outfit on, all the other members had kente cloth on. Thus even though the cloth was known in some circles, it was leaders like Nkrumah who helped to introduce it in the international forum. On such occasions, while everyone else maintained the status quo (three-piece suit or tuxedo), Kwame Nkrumah and his followers fully draped themselves in kente. By the early 1960s the cloth had gained popularity in America in the form of a stole or scarf worn around the neck over a dress or a coat symbolizing a renewed pride of Afrikan heritage. Kente cloth and fugu or batakiri (dashiki) became the outfit with which one could easily, simply, and proudly enhance the hidden negroid beauty.

Why Kente Cloth?

It will be misleading to say that kente is the only Afrikan material known and used in America or other parts of the world that can be identified with Afrikans. There are certainly other fabrics which are associated with particular ethnic groups in Afrika. For example the Mud-cloth from Mali, Tie-Dye, and Akwete from Nigeria, and Adinkra-cloth from Ghana plus many more that are originated from the continent. The question here is why has kente gain more prominence in the apparel industry worldwide today than the others. The simplest answer to this question is economic and social factors are responsible for that. Economically, there is demand and supply for the cloth. And socially, its intrinsic value and charisma as already discussed in other chapters make kente cloth an ideal product. Looking at America alone, one sees in almost every major city, dozens of

Afrikan novelty stores have risen up selling kente cloth. An example of this is Ghanam Textiles Inc., a New York based company that imports many kinds of Afrikan fabrics including kente cloth, and produces outfits and accessories for national distribution. Kente cloth is the accepted medium through which our pride in Afrikan culture is transmitted. The cloth has helped to bridge the gap between black people of the world regardless of their nationality or background. It is like a buckle that fastens black America with black Afrika. It has become the most visible Afrikan image carrier that clearly spells out "the Afrikan awareness statement". Today as it was yesterday, with kente-cloth, it is no guess that the wearer is conscious of Afrikan roots. The cloth has always served the public as its messenger in disguise. It can simply be classified as the umbilical cord that links mother Afrika with all her children across this planet.

It purifies the Afrikan personality. The beauty of Kente cloth bestows on its wearer dignity, pride, and wisdom that is unmatched by anything else of Afrikan origin.

Magnetic Effects of Kente Cloth

A recent observation in USA shows that kente cloth is not limited to the apparel industry only, but it is also used by corporations and some official institutions, obviously as a magnet, to attract the black audience. A Federal organization such as the Post Office used a picture of Adjwini Asa kente pattern as a magnet to promote the sale of its specialized collectors postage stamps "The US Postal Services Proudly Presents 'I have a dream.' A collection of Black Americans on US postage Stamps" in January 1992. Again in early December 1991, a 70 year white Judge in Washington DC told a black lawyer in court to take off his Kente strip which he was wearing around his neck at the time, because the Judge thought the cloth would influence the decision of the jury. The lawyer maintained that he was a member of a religious group which expected all its officers to wear kente strips around the neck at all public appearances to symbolize unity among church members and their pride in Afrikan culture. The Judge further threatened to remove the lawyer from the court if his directives were ignored. In his reply, the lawyer insisted that he would rather apply to have the case tried by another judge. The main point here is that the traditional face value of kente cloth was clearly well exposed by the judge and the lawyer. The precise pattern of kente he was wearing at the time may not be really pertinent, what mattered then was the fact that the cloth was known to have an intrinsic quality to transmit messages. Corporate America has accepted kente cloth as the Afrikan cloth. It is no more shameful to appear in public or a nine-to-five environment with a kente neck-tie or scarf over a jacket. In fact it is fashionable these days to see invited guests attending to office parties in kente cummerbund and bow-tie or suspenders matching set. It is common these days to go to departmental stores such as J.C. Penny, Macy's, A&S, Bloomingdales, and many more across the country to find a product which is made with kente cloth or with the look of a kente pattern. The massmedia particularly the press has shown much interest in exposing to the general public why kente is seen everywhere in America and where it comes from. *The New York Times* for example has never ceased to probe and to inform its readers anything new about the cloth that comes to their office. *The Wall Street Journal, The Amsterdam News, Ebony Magazine, Essence Magazine* and several thousands of written works are only a few who have shown tremendous admiration of this great Afrikan artwork of antiquity. Any work on kente cloth will not be complete without mentioning the wonderful show of solidarity and brotherhood of the hundreds of religious organizations, fraternities, schools, colleges, and universities who have helped to put kente-cloth the all-afrikan-cloth in its rightful place on the globe. It is pitiful though that Ghanaians in Ghana do not see this picture.

Chapter Seven
KENTE IDEOLOGY
TRADITIONALIST & NON-TRADITIONALIST

This topic deals with notions and perceptions that surround kente cloth. Kente as an economic good, kente as a mere Afrikan fabric for fashion, and kente as a banner symbolizing African craftmanship and concepts.

Traditionalist

This may be defined as someone who believes in strict observance of customs and traditions without distortions. A traditionalist maintains status quo regardless of changing circumstances or social situations. His perception of kente cloth would be any of the following or both:

a). Kente is an important Ashanti treasure hence none of the classic patterns should be altered in any form for any reason. It looses its traditional image if it has no name or significance. All kente immitations must be rejected.

b). The cloth must be purposefully used only on special occasions by distinguished people, especially citizens who have excelled to high ranks such as kings, chiefs, leaders, and elderstatesmen. Men should drape the cloth around the body as it is customarily worn by the Ashantis with the bare chest exposed in a mgnificient form; ie, wearing kente over another attire covering ones chest like the Fantis or Ewes is untraditional. Only females should be seen to wear kente over another dress.

c) A traditionalist detests the use of the cloth as an accessory product such as baseball caps, bowtie, dansiki, shoes etc. etc. It is believed that by so treating the cloth, it would lose its importance and therefore become an object of mediocrity and scorn.

Non-traditionalist

A non-traditionalist rejects all the ancient kente culture and redefines its functional role in modern day Ashanti and the rest of the world. His vision of the cloth is much broader and real than the traditionalist. He sees *kente as a royal and a regal product.* For example regally, one need not be a king, a chief, a member of a royal family, a statesman, a rich parson, or a VIP to use a kente cloth. As long as you have a desire to look at your best, you are qualified enough to wear kente at anytime, anywhere, anyhow according to this school of thought. He sees the cloth beyond its original narrow intentions. It plays a multi-purpose role instead. It is a beauty enhancer of the Afrikan personality. It purifies his black image with distinction. It transmitts his ethical messages silently and effectively. And because of such visual qualities, and a belief that anybody can use the cloth, it does not matter to him whether the cloth is genuine hand-woven Ashanti-made or not. It may be a kente-print, a machine-weave kente, or a hand-weave kente made in Keta, Abidjan, Darkar, Stevenage, Toronto, New York or Bonwire : the kind or source of the cloth is not important to a nontraditionalist. The material could be cut into pieces to make an outfit or accessories such as caps, hats, shirts, ties, sunglasses, skirts, blouses, pants, socks, shoes, bags, curtains, bedspreads, etc. etc. The important feature expected is the pattern of the cloth. It must have the usual kente pictograms and geometric shapes and be very colorful. This notion accepts the basic concepts of the material and stretches it to embrace all classes of people to suit modern universal conditions. Thus eliminating the ethinc snobbery between Afrikans everywhere. He uses kente anywhere anyhow because it identifies him or her quickly with the motherland without a word of mouth. The cloth over-rides all nationality tags which all Afrikans everywhere have been labeled by incidence of history. By this token, there is no need to know the meaning or significance of the kente he or she has on. The cloth is the history. It assures you that you are a natural brother or sister in theory and appearance. A member of a lost generation who truely feels proud to claim back this hidden heritage. Kente is no more an Ashanti traditional cloth, it is certainly an international cloth that represents all Afrikans. Kente is simply an Afrikan cloth. Brothers and sisters who got spirited away from the motherland accidentally can justly claim the pride and joy of the cloth in the same manner an Ashanti can. According to a non traditionalist the cloth belong to all people of Afrikan descent.

A Discussion of Kente Ideology

Ghanaians in general and Ashantis in particular can be classified as traditionalist. They detest the idea of using kente cloth for hats, dansiki, shoe and any outfit that deviates from the norm. Even the highly educated citizens who could be expected to have been influenced by foreign culture are very adamant about any interferance with kente traditions. Most Ashantis interviewed believe that the recent increase in its immitation will eventually lead to defamation of an important treasure which has passed on to them from generation to future generations. They foresee the end of an era when kente was considered as their number one property among all personal wealth. The few non-traditionalist Ghanaians appear to be less concerned about its usage, but more worried about how others are manipulating the cloth to exploit black Afrika. An oldman in Kumasi (Ashanti capital) sums it up beautifully as follows: "It is business as usual isn't it? First they came with sword and crucifix, they went back with our able men and women. They came back again for our gold, timber, and cocoa in exchange for their schnapps, pen, and bogus culture. Now they are back again for the only one thing we have left – our kente cloth. I hope they will not claim they invented it for us as they have done with many of our inventions." The fear of kente being taken away from Ghanaians is not wide spread but there seems to be some substance in it. Export of kente materials from West Afrikan countries to America is growing at a faster rate because there is an increased demand for them. According to 1990 USA population count, there are 29,986,060 Black Persons in the United States as per US Census Bureau. This figure represents 12% of the overall population. It further states that the growth rate of this population is greater than all other ethnic groups, about 13% compared to 6% among whites during 1980-1990 period. The inference we can draw from this is that if kente cloth is mainly consumed by American Blacks and their numbers are increasing, there exist a possibility that supply and demand of kente will continue to increase assuming the purpose for which it is supplied and demanded remains constant or gets better. The economic and social mutual benefits on both sides of the Atlantic is obvious. Socially, a greater use of kente will help to raise the level of awareness and cohesion among Blacks in America. And economically, the Afrikan countries engaged in production of kente cloth will benefit through employment and income at every level of the trade. While a non-traditionalist see this as the inevitable result of the kente connection, the traditionalist perceives it with pessimism. He believes that manufacturers of other fabrics in other countries will suffer from the shift in demand from their goods to those produced in Afrika. This may force some manufacturers particularly cotton prints and other colorful materials producers out of business or rather push them to convert their existing plants to manufacture kente materials. This will not be a healthy competition for the Afrikan kente producers. The handweavers may not be affected in the short term. It will not be surprising in the future if someone comes out with an automated loom to weave the Ashanti four-inch norrow strips at a fraction of the current price. Those producing kente immitation fabrics are potential loosers in the forseable future, because their foreign competitors can either buy them off the market at a stroke or evict them slowly by dumping cheap immitations into the market. Pakistan is already exporting immitations of the immitation kente prints to the American market (front part of fabric shows the look of kente, the back side fades out). Taiwan is producing nylon with kente look for umbrella, swim-wear ect. ect. And this is seen only as the beginning. The survival of the Afrikan manufacturers can be sustained only if the American consumer can identify the difference or will learn to differentiate between what is *authentic* Afrikan fabric and what is not. The traditionalist does not however see this as happening soon, because most people care much about the looks than the traditional substance. Considering the abundance of technology and capital and the size of the market, it will not be too long that these fears will become real; and when it does, the monetary benefits will not be enjoyed by the Afrikan brothers. It will definitely have a U-turn shape. Economically therefore, it will not be in the best interest of indigenous Afrikans to persue the non-traditionalist views of kente *(use anykind, anyhow, anywhere, anytime);* unless of-course the social benefits can off-set these economic pitfalls or rather transform itself somehow into other economic ventures directly in Afrika to resurrect the industries. There are some indications in the tourist sector in recent years which can be interpreted as positive effects of the non-traditionalist approach. Scores of brothers and sisters are visiting the motherland more frequently than ever before, mainly to solidify the renewed awareness as a primary stage towards the inevitable unification of kith-and-kins of Afrika.

Chapter Eight

MOST POPULAR QUESTIONS AND ANSWERS ABOUT KENTE CLOTH

Q: What is kente?

A: Kente is an Ashanti traditional hand-loom-woven designer cloth. It is made of fine colorful yarns into narrow strips in geometric patterns. The size of a typical strip is approximately 4x72 inches for female and 4x144 inches for male.

Q: From where does it originate?

A: Kente cloth is known to originate from Ashanti Region of Ghana.

Q: Is it true that kente is woven by men only?

A: No, it is incorrect to say that only men can or do weave kente. There are several known women at Bonwire and elsewhere who are capable of weaving even some of the most difficult patterns. It is true however that it used to be made only by men before the end of the second world war.

Q: Is it possible that kente cloth could have come from some part of Afrika?

A: Yes it is possible; yet we must maintain the established wisdom that the Ashanti people of Ghana created it until it is thoroughly researched and proven beyond all reasonable doubts. Afrikan textiles and fabrics in general have attracted a few writers since the beginning of this century and it has been documented in many areas that in almost every distinct Afrikan ethnic group, there is available a unique type of a loom-woven cloth. It is noted also that most of the Afrikan fabrics are similar in many ways, but the finished products are never identical to each other. We must therefore avoid simple equation of their similarities with their differences.

Q: Can men and women of any age use kente pattern of any kind?

A: Yes, even though initially it was adult men only. Kyemea kente for example was designed with female in mind, but both sexes of all ages have used it throughout the years. In Nkrumah's famous portrait, he is wearing kyemea. *Refer to picture 4.*

Q: Can kente be used at any time anywhere?

A: Yes. Even though kente was traditionally made for occasional use by the aristocracy only, modern historical experiences has upgraded kente's status to that of an ambassador representing all black people every time everywhere.

Q: What is the significance of kente?

A: Kente exposes the hidden Afrikan personality and glorifies it with distinguished beauty, dignity, pride and wisdom.

Q: Is it necessary to know the meaning of a kente pattern before using it?

A: No. It is not necessary. Because even in Ashanti where kente originated, there is only about two in every hundred people who will be able to tell the meaning of a single kente pattern. Even among the modern as opposed to traditional weavers, there is only a fraction who could narrate the true history or meaning of all the patterns he weaves. Most of buyers and sellers in Ghana can tell the names of most patterns, but not their significance. It is essential however to be able to differentiate between the Ashanti traditional kente from all others. Because it is only those that carry traditional names and histories. It should be emphasized that there are several anonymous beautiful designs available that have no particular traditional meaning whatsoever, yet they carry the same kente philosophy. Again someone with the knowledge of authentic Ashanti kente will be able to make educated choices when exposed with a variety of the cloth.

Q: Are there imitations of kente cloth?

A: Yes. There are many kinds. All handwoven kente that are not consistent with the Ashanti traditional patterns are considered as imitations. Even among the imitations, there are copies that look real. *Refer to "Other forms of kente cloth" topic for more information.*

Q: Is it wrong to wear kente print or any imitation kente cloth?

A: The answer is No and Yes, depending on whether you are a traditionalist or non-traditionalist. If you say No, there is nothing wrong with that, because all kente cloth, regardless of their source is a universal Afrikan cloth which facilitates the promotion of the Afrikan image, you are considered a non-traditionalist. A traditionalist will say Yes it is wrong to use any imitation kente. He rejects all forms of kente apart from the real Ashanti classic patterns, and he uses them when it is required of him to deliver a specific message to a specific audience. *Please refer to "Kente Ideology" topic.*

Q: Do colors in kente cloth have special meaning ?

A: Not necessarily so. Some Kente cloth designs are made with specific colors and weavers throughout ages have been very consistent with these original colors. For example, Sika Futro and Adjwini Asa have always been predominantly yellow, with other supporting colors like wine, red, black, green, and seldom blue. And in almost all kentes, white thread is always used as a dividing line between block patterns. The yellow color in sika futro represents wealth, riches, or gold which Ashantis pride themselves with. (Over 98% of all Ghana's natural deposit of Gold is located in the region.) Wine and red colors are almost universally associated with blood and toil of human experience, or very often used to symbolize readiness to resort to violence when necessary; blue as an agent for tranquility; and green representing earthly sustenance. And white boarders showing peaceful intervals which is akin to all mankind. Color combination in kente has never been clearly spelled out, but in the process of creating new patterns, most weavers interviewed appear to have such ideas as explained above in mind.

Q: Kinta, Kinte, Kunta, Kinti — Are these proper names or descriptions of Kente cloth?

A: No. None of the above names or descriptions have anything to do with kente cloth. Some people often spell kente wrongly as one the above. These words may mean something but they should not be used in reference to kente cloth in any way.

GLOSSARY

Twi Words and their Meaning

Abidjan (french): Capital of Ivory Coast

Abodin: Honorary Title

Abrempong-Ntoma:
A pompous style of draping cloth

Abusua-ye-dom: A famous kente pattern;
family at loggerheads

Adinkra: Last-farewell
(name of Ashanti printed fabric)

Adjwini: Design, Brains, Concept

Adjwini-asa: End of Design. Famous kente
pattern.

Adjwini - Nwenentoma: Designer - woven cloth (Kente-Cloth)

Aduana: One of seven clans in Ghana

Ahwepan: Ordinary/Plain woven cloth

Ankh (Egyptian): An emblem of life

Asa: Ended, Accomplished, Completed

Asakyiri: One of seven clans in Ghana

Asante: A person of Ashanti descent; their language

Asantehene: King/ruler of Asante people

Asase-Ntoma: The apprentice or children woven fabric

Aseneye: One of seven clans in Ghana

Asesia: One-of-a-kind Asantehene's Kente

Ashanti: A region in Ghana

Asona: One of seven clans in Ghana

Aso-oke: A Yoruba hand-loom woven cloth

Batakari: Moshie traditional garment. Dashiki

Bonwire: Most ancient kente-weaving village.

Bratuo: One of seven clans in Ghana

Dansiki: Correct Yoruba name for dashiki outfit; a loose shirt or pullover,

Dansi-nkran: Ashanti women traditional hair-do

Dashiki: A popular name in US for Dansiki

Dua sika: A plant used for making yellow color

Dubumaa: A plant used for black coloring.

Ekuona: One of seven clans in Ghana.

Emmaa-da: Never-occured. A famous kente pattern

Epepiakyire/Epiakyire: Fortress. A famous kente pattern.

Essumja: One of traditional areas/town in Ashanti

Eti-kro-nko-agyina: One-head-does-not-form-a-committee; famous kente pattern.

Fatia-fata-Nkrumah: Fathia befits Nkrumah as a spouse. Recently (1957-60) created kente pattern

Francis Nkrumah: Dr. Kwame Nkrumah's original name

Fugu: Moshie traditional loom-woven material

Ghana: Country in W. Afrika. Home of Kente.

Hene: King/Chief

Henemaa/Ohenmaa: Queen/Queenmother

Kasie Dua: Name of plant/tree for red color

Kente: Asante designer woven cloth

Kɛ`nte (kernte): Kente old spelling

Kɛ`ntɛ`n (kerntern): A basket. Asante word for

Kɛ`tɛ`(kerter): A mat. Asante word for

Kente-hene: Kente-chief. Head of Ashanti kenteweavers.

Keta: A town in Volta region Ghana.

Kinta, Kinte, Kinti, Kunta: Wrong spellings of Kente.

Kumasi: Capital city of Ashanti region. Ghana.

Kumawu: Ashanti traditional town/area

Kyemia: A famous kente pattern for queen-mothers.

Mampam-se/Nanka-tiri: Reptille's teeth or its head. Recently commissioned kente pattern. Design for highly articulate but often despised people

Manhyia: Ex-capital of Asante (Official Residence of King of Asante)

Nana: Excellence, maturity title for kings/queens

Nana Ameyaw: One of two legends who invented kente

Nana Koragu: One of two legends who invented kente

Nana Kwame Gyabi-Ababio: Ex-Traditional Chief of Essumja Ashanti

Nana Otaa-Kraban: Creator of classic kente pattern "Oyoko-man"

Nsadua: The loom. Wooden-frame locally built for weaving cloth.

Ntoma: A cloth

Ntoma-ban: A kente cloth strip

Nwene: Weave or Woven

Nwene-ntoma: A woven cloth

Oba-djwini-ba: A thinker, a creator, an inventor.

Okanii-ba: A nickname for a full-blooded Asante

Okatakyie: One of Asantehene's titles. His greatness His invincibility.

Oke`sie`: A responsible, great, and praise-worthy man.

Onwine-ma-hene: Kings-weaver

Opanin: A distinguished/honorable elderly man

Osagyefo: The mightiest

Otumfuo: One of Asantehene's titles. His prowess, wisdom, and respectability

Oyoko: One of seven clans in Ghana

Oyoko-mma: A classic kente pattern designed by Otaa Kraban of Bonwire for chief spokesman of oyoko-clan (Nana Asantehene)

Sesia-adaka: Asantehene's treasure box containing rare kente patterns

Sika-futro: Gold-powder. Famous kente pattern.

Serikye: Silk

Twi: Language of Akan people or Asante.

Akan First Names

First names are obtained according to the day of the week one is born.

DAY	MALE		FEMALE	
	ASANTE	OTHERS	ASANTE	OTHERS
Sunday	Akwasi	Kwesi	Akosua	Esi
Monday	Kwadjwo	Jojo	Adjoa	Ajoa
Tuesday	Kwabena	Kobina	Abena	Aba
Wednesday	Kwaku	Kweku	Akua	Ekua
Thursday	Yaw	Kow	Yaa	Yaa
Friday	Kofi	Fifi	Afua	Efua
Saturday	Kwame	Kwami	Amma	Ama

About the author

Born 1948 in a small village called Abodom located at the southeastern part of Bekwai in Ashanti Region Ghana. Completed the first five year elementary education in the village Methodist School and Bekwai S.D.A middle school for the remaining five years ending in 1958. Migrated to England in 1965 and graduated from University of London with a Bachelor of Science Degree in Economics. Worked as Administrative Officer in the Ghana civil service between 1976 and 1980. Migrated to US in 1980 where he learnt that his personal interest in Afrikan culture, particularly that of Akan, was not an isolated case. That the culture was already accepted and integrated in America.As a Ghanian, an Ashanti, and a merchant in Afrikan fabrics and artifact, he believes he is qualified enough to write and to share with the public his knowledge of that culture which has become almost synonymous universally with Afrkan culture in general.